OTHER HELEN EXLEY GIFTBOOKS:
Wisdom for Our Times
Words on Hope
Words on Love and Caring
Thank You for Every Little Thing

First published 1998. Published in this format 2001, 2006.
Copyright © Helen Exley 1998, 2001, 2006.
The moral right of the author has been asserted.

12 11 10 9 8 7 6 5 4 3 2 1

Edited and pictures selected by Helen Exley
ISBN 1-84634-048-9

Printed in China.

Helen Exley Giftbooks, 16 Chalk Hill, Watford,
Herts WD19 4BG, UK.
Helen Exley Giftbooks LLC, 185 Main Street, Spencer,
MA 01562, USA.
www.helenexleygiftbooks.com

Words on
Calm

A HELEN EXLEY GIFTBOOK

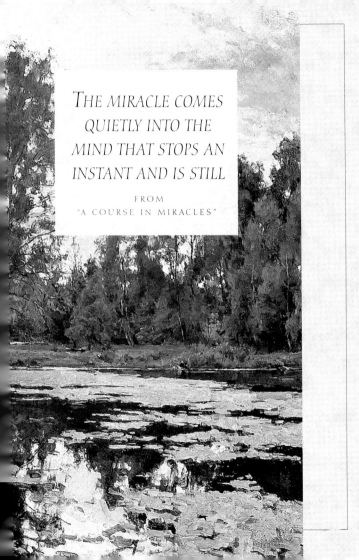

THE MIRACLE COMES
QUIETLY INTO THE
MIND THAT STOPS AN
INSTANT AND IS STILL

FROM
"A COURSE IN MIRACLES"

*Contentment...
comes as the infallible
result of great
acceptances, great
humilities –
of not trying to make
ourselves this or that
(to conform
to some dramatized
version of ourselves),
but of surrendering
ourselves to the
fullness of life –
of letting life
flow through us.*

DAVID GRAYSON

Why should we live with such hurry and waste of life? ... Men say that a stitch in time saves nine, and so they take a thousand stitches today to save nine tomorrow. As for work, we haven't any of any consequence. We have Saint Vitus' dance, and cannot possibly keep our heads still.

HENRY DAVID THOREAU
(1817-1862)

*L*isten in deep silence.
Be very still and open
your mind....
Sink deep into the peace that
waits for you beyond
the frantic, riotous thoughts
and sights and sounds
of this insane world.

FROM "A COURSE IN MIRACLES"

*Serenity is neither
frivolity, nor complacency,
it is the highest knowledge
and love, it is the
affirmation of all reality
being awake at the edge
of all deeps and abysses.
Serenity is the secret
of beauty and the real
substance of all art.*

HERMANN HESSE
(1877-1962)

THE SERENE

HAVE NOT OPTED OUT

OF LIFE.

THEY SEE MORE WIDELY,

LOVE MORE DEARLY,

REJOICE IN THE THINGS

THE FRANTIC MIND

NO LONGER SEES

OR HEARS.

PAM BROWN, b.1928

Leave home in the sunshine:
Dance through a meadow –
Or sit by a stream
and just be.
The lilt of the water
Will gather your worries
And carry them down
to the sea.

J DONALD WALTERS

*Serenity does not
cancel hope or adventure,
work or love.
It flows through the landscape
of our busy lives,
quiet and strong.
Clear and gentle.
Refreshing all we do
or dream.*

PAM BROWN, b 1928

*W*ork is not always required of a man. There is such a thing as sacred idleness, the cultivation of which is now fearfully neglected.

GEORGE MACDONALD (1824-1905)

IF YOU CAN SPEND A PERFECTLY USELESS AFTERNOON IN A PERFECTLY USELESS MANNER, YOU HAVE LEARNED HOW TO LIVE.

LIN YUTANG (1895-1976)

*P*eace is the
fairest form of
happiness.

WILLIAM ELLERY CHANNING
(1780-1842)

*Teach me the art
of creating islands
of stillness,
in which I can absorb
the beauty of
everyday things:
clouds, trees, a snatch
of music....*

Don't hurry don't worry,
you're only here
for a short visit.
So be sure to stop
and smell the flowers.

WALTER HAGAN

Whatever peace I know
rests in the natural world,
in feeling myself a part of it,
even in a small way.

MAY SARTON,
FROM "JOURNAL OF A SOLITUDE"

OUR GREATEST EXPERIENCES
ARE OUR QUIETEST MOMENTS.

NIETZSCHE
(1844-1900)

*Happiness is
as a butterfly, which,
when pursued, is always
beyond our grasp,
but which, if you will
sit down quietly, may alight
upon you.*

NATHANIEL HAWTHORNE
(1804-1864)

*The way to use life
is to do nothing
through acting. The way
to use life is to do
everything through being.*

LAO-TZU

Do not let trifles
disturb your tranquillity
of mind....
Life is too precious
to be sacrificed for
the nonessential
and transient....
Ignore the inconsequential.

GRENVILLE KLEISER

There is, perhaps, no solitary sensation so exquisite as that of slumbering on the grass or hay, shaded from the hot sun by a tree, with the consciousness of a fresh light air running through the wide atmosphere, and the sky stretching far overhead upon all sides.

LEIGH HUNT
(1784-1859)

Deep in the soul, below pain,
below all the distraction of life,
is a silence vast and grand –
an infinite ocean of calm,
which nothing can disturb;
Nature's own exceeding peace,
which "passes understanding".
That which we seek with
passionate longing,
here and there, upward and
outward; we find at last
within ourselves.

C.M.C. QUOTED BY R.M. BUCKE

*T*here is no quiet place
in the white man's cities,
no place to hear the leaves
of spring or the rustle
of insects' wings....
The Indians prefer the soft
sound of the wind
darting over the face
of the pond, the smell
of the wind itself cleansed
by the midday rain,
or scented with pinion pine.

CHIEF SEATTLE

Life just is. You have
to flow with it. Give
yourself to the moment.
Let it happen.

GOVERNOR JERRY BROWN

*A*rranging a bowl
of flowers in the morning
can give a sense of quiet
in a crowded day –
like writing a poem,
or saying a prayer.

ANNE MORROW LINDBERGH

Here will we sit
and let the sounds
of music creep in our ears:
soft stillness and the night
become the touches of
sweet harmony.

WILLIAM SHAKESPEARE
(1564-1616)

THE QUIETER
YOU BECOME,
THE MORE
YOU CAN HEAR.

BABA RAM DASS

If we are not happy,
if we are not peaceful,
we cannot share peace
and happiness with others,
even those we love, those
who live under the same roof.
If we are peaceful,
if we are happy, we can smile
and blossom like a flower,
and everyone in our family,
our entire society, will
benefit from our peace.

THICH NHAT HANH

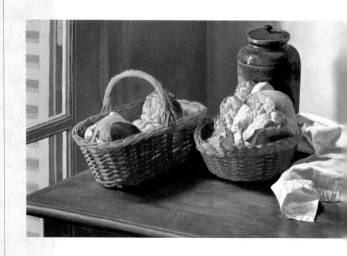

When I set myself sometimes to consider the divers agitations of men, and the troubles and dangers to which they expose themselves.... I see that all their misfortunes come from one thing only, that they know not how to dwell in peace, in a room.

BLAISE PASCAL
(1623-1662)

*O*ver all the mountaintops

Is peace.

In all treetops

You perceive

Scarcely a breath.

The little birds in the forest

Are silent.

Wait then; soon

You, too, will have peace.

JOHANN WOLFGANG
VON GOETHE
(1749-1832)

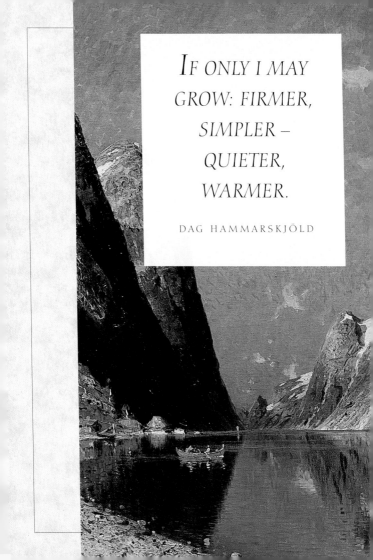

IF ONLY I MAY GROW: FIRMER, SIMPLER – QUIETER, WARMER.

DAG HAMMARSKJÖLD

I lay in a meadow
until the unwrinkled serenity
entered into my bones,
and made me into one
with the browsing kine,
the still greenery,
the drifting clouds,
and the swooping birds.

ALICE JAMES

I expand and live
in the warm day
like corn and melons.

RALPH WALDO EMERSON
(1803-1882)

*Peace is not
something you wish for;
it's something you make,
something you do,
something you are, and
something you give away!*

ROBERT FULGHUM

Serenity is active.
It is a gentle and firm
participation with trust.
Serenity is the relaxation
of our cells into who we are
and a quiet celebration
of that relaxation.

ANNE WILSON SCHAEF

Peace is not a passive
but an active condition,
not a negation but an
affirmation. It is a gesture
as strong as war.

MARY ROBERTS RINEHART

*C*ome away from the din.
Come away to the quiet fields,
over which the great sky stretches,
and where, between us
and the stars, there lies

but silence; and there,
in the stillness let us listen
to the voice that is speaking
within us.

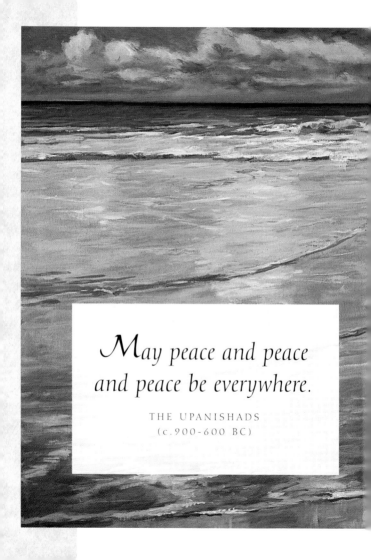

*M*ay peace and peace
and peace be everywhere.

THE UPANISHADS
(c.900-600 BC)

The quiet mind
is richer than
a crown.
... Such sweet
content, such minds,
such sleep,
such bliss
Beggars enjoy
when princes oft
do miss.

ROBERT GREENE
(1558-1592)

My greatest wealth
is the deep stillness
in which I strive and grow
and win what the world
cannot take from me
with fire or sword.

JOHANN WOLFGANG VON GOETHE
(1749-1832)

The poor long
for riches and the rich
for heaven, but the wise
long for a state
of tranquillity.

SWAMI RAMA

Ultimately we have just
one moral duty: to reclaim
large areas of peace
in ourselves, more and more
peace, and to reflect it
toward others. And the more
peace there is in us, the more
peace there will be in
our troubled world.

ETTY HILLESUM

*P*EACE IS INEVITABLE
TO THOSE WHO OFFER PEACE.

FROM "A COURSE IN MIRACLES"

*The strong, calm man
is always loved and revered.
He is like a shade-giving tree
in a thirsty land,
or a sheltering rock
in a storm.*

JAMES ALLEN (1864-1912)

FROM SERENITY
COMES
GENTLENESS,
COMES
LASTING STRENGTH.

PAM BROWN, b.1928

To a mind
that is still
the whole universe
surrenders.

CHUANG TZU

Too many people, too
many demands, too much
to do; competent, busy,
hurrying people –
It just isn't living at all.

*Life is eating us up.
We shall be fables
presently. Keep cool:
it will be all one
a hundred years hence.*

RALPH WALDO EMERSON
(1803-1882)

*And so, while others
miserably pledge
themselves to the
insatiable pursuit
of ambition and*

BRIEF POWER, I WILL

BE STRETCHED OUT

IN THE SHADE, SINGING.

FRAY LUIS DE LEÓN (c.1527–1591)

What life can compare to this? Sitting quietly by the window, I watch the leaves fall and the flowers bloom, as the seasons come and go.

HSUEH-TOU (980-1052)

*B*efore me peaceful
Behind me peaceful
Under me peaceful
Over me peaceful
Around me peaceful

NAVAJO PRAYER

Acknowledgements: The publishers are grateful for permission to reproduce copyright material. Whilst every reasonable effort has been made to trace copyright holders, the publishers would be pleased to hear from any not here acknowledged. THICH NHAT HANH: From *Being Peace* (1987) by Thich Nhat Hanh with permission from Parallax Press, Berkeley, California. ETTY HILLESUM: From *An Interrupted Life – The Diaries of Etty Hillesum 1941-1943.* ANNE MORROW LINDBERGH: From *Bring Me A Unicorn,* published by Harcourt Brace Jovanovich, 1971, 1972 by Anne Morrow Lindbergh. J. DONALD WALTERS: From *"There's Joy in the Heavens",* published by Crystal Clarity Publishers. PAM BROWN: © Helen Exley 1998, 2001, 2006.

Picture credits: Helen Exley Giftbooks would like to thank the following organizations and individuals for permission to reproduce their pictures. Whilst every reasonable effort has been made to trace the copyright holders, the publishers would be pleased to hear from any not here acknowledged. Archiv für Kunst (AKG), Artworks (AW), Bridgeman Art Library (BAL), Fine Art Photographic Library (FAP), Giraudon (GIR), Index (IND), SuperStock (SS).

Cover: © Richard Exley; title page: Claude Monet, *Waterlilies;* pages 6/7: Valentin Alexandrovitch Serov, *Pond in Thicket,* AKG; pages 8/9: © 1998 Walter Farmer, *Through a Window,* BAL; page 10: Norbert Goeneutte, *Doctor Paul Gachet,* GIR; page 12: Matias Morales, *Columbian Woman on a Divan,* SS; page 14: Gamaliel Subang, *Dining Table;* page 16: © 1998 Florence Eden, *The Little Weaver,* SS; page 19:

Aleksandr Andreevic Ivanov, *Water and Stones,* SS; page 21: Edouard Dubufe, *Portrait of Juliette Dubufe,* GIR; page 23: Eugene Boudin, *Trouville: The Pier,* GIR; pages 24/25: Pierre Auguste Renoir, *Summer Landscape,* BAL; page 26: Karoly Ferenczy, *Bird Song,* BAL; page 29: © 1998 Harold Speed, *The Garden Path,* SS; page 30: James Jacques Joseph Tissot, *Reverie: Mrs Newton Reclining in a Chair,* BAL; page 33: Berga I. Boix, *Countryside,* IND; pages 34/35: Elliot Clark, *Cold Spring Harbor;* page 37: Jean Hippolyle Flandrin, *Nude Young Man At The Seaside,* GIR; page 39: © 1998 Gyokudo Kawai, *Summer Shower,* BAL; pages 40/41: Timothy Easton, *Morning Break,* BAL; page 43: © 1998 Karen Armitage, *Agapanthus Molucela Arrangement in a Glass Vase,* BAL; page 44: John Atkinson Grimshaw, *Moonlight on the Lake, Roundhay Park,* FAP; page 47: *Home Sweet Home;* page 48: 1998 Juan Lascano, *Baskets of Bread,* SS; page 50: Paul Cezanne, *The Bridge At Maincy,* GIR/BAL; pages 52/53: Adelsteen Normann, *Reflections in a Norwegian Fjord,* FAP; page 55: © 1998 Charles Neal, *River Nene,* SS; page 56: © 1998 Dame Laura Knight, *Summertime, Cornwall,* BAL; pages 58/59: John Ruskin, *Stormy Sunset,* BAL; pages 60/61: John Hollis Kaufmann, *Sea Change,* SS; page 62: © 1998 Rose Mary Barton, *The Haycart Approaches,* BAL; page 65: © 1998 Joel Spector, AW; page 66: J.S. Chardin, *Portrait of Jacques Aved,* GIR; page 68: Private Collection; pages 70/71: Vincent Van Gogh, *Garden of Daubigny;* page 73: © 1998 Alberto Pisa, *Holmwood, Surrey,* BAL; pages 74/75: Claude Monet, *Waterlilies.*